How to Use Debt

Jackson Cooper

Copyright Page

Publisher: Dakini

Release Year 2025

Index

Copyright Page

Publisher: Dakini

Index

Debt Is Not Your Enemy

For a long time, debt has been viewed as a kind of financial monster to be avoided at all costs. We were taught to fear it, to reject it, to see it as a sign of failure or irresponsibility. It has become a word that many people prefer not to mention, as if it were something shameful. But the truth is that debt, in and of itself, is neither good nor bad. It's simply a tool. And like any tool, it all depends on how you use it.

Imagine a knife. In the hands of a chef, a knife is used to create exquisite dishes. In inexperienced or careless hands, it can cause accidents. The same is true of debt. Used wisely and with planning, it can help you grow financially, achieve goals faster, invest in your education, start a business, or buy a home. Used without control or knowledge, it can become a burden that prevents you from moving forward.

Many people who are financially free or wealthy today started out using debt. What will make the difference is whether that debt was used to purchase assets or liabilities. Buying liabilities with debt—like clothes, gadgets, vacations, or things that lose value—usually leads to problems. But borrowing money to invest in something that will generate income, grow in value over time, or increase your personal productivity is a completely different story.

The key is purpose. Why are you taking on that debt? If the answer is emotional—because "I deserve it," because "I don't want to wait," because "everyone does it"—you're probably walking into a trap. But if the answer is rational, if you've done the math and know that debt will get you closer to a realistic, measurable goal, then you may be making a smart financial move.

Debt can open doors. It can accelerate your progress. You don't need to wait ten years to raise the money you need to study for a degree or launch a business if you can access a loan that allows you to do it today. Sure, it involves risk. But so does living. And any risk that's calculated and backed by a good plan can be a worthwhile gamble.

What you need to avoid is the impulsive and unconscious use of debt. It's not about going into debt for the sake of it, or accumulating credit cards as trophies. It's about learning to use debt as a strategy. Understanding the rules of the game, knowing how much you're going to pay, how long it will take, and what real benefit you'll get from that money that isn't yours, but that you can use to your advantage.

There are people who have built empires thanks to credit. Giant companies that started with loans. Homeowners who bought their first property with borrowed money and now have a real estate portfolio. Entrepreneurs who used a loan to buy machinery, hire staff, and multiply their income. They didn't achieve this because debt was magical, but because they knew what they were doing.

But there are also those who go into debt without knowing how they'll repay, without reading the terms, without understanding what they're signing. And then they blame the debt. It's not the money borrowed that's to blame, but the misuse of it. Therefore, rather than rejecting debt, what we need to do is understand it, learn to use it as a valuable resource.

Thinking that all debt is bad is like thinking that all fire burns. Yes, fire can burn, but it can also cook, provide warmth, and light. The problem isn't the fire itself, it's how you use it. The same goes for debt. If you educate yourself financially, if you learn to read contracts, if you do your math, if you plan and maintain control, debt won't be your enemy. On the contrary, it can become one of your greatest allies as you move forward in life.

And this is where the real change in mindset begins. Because what you've perhaps been taught is to fear, avoid, and hide from debt. But what you need now is to understand and master it. Stop seeing it as a threat and start seeing it as a possibility. If you do this right, debt won't trap you. It will push you forward.

This book isn't about how to get deeper into debt, but about how to do it better. It's about changing your relationship with borrowed money and becoming a person who not only knows how to manage their finances, but also knows how to use them strategically. Because when you use debt wisely, it's no longer a burden. It's a lever that propels you to achieve what once seemed impossible.

Types of Debt

Not all debt is created equal. Just as not all jobs, relationships, or decisions have the same impact on your life, debt also comes in different shapes, sizes, and consequences. And if you're going to use it, it's vital that you know exactly what you're dealing with. Identifying the types of debt is like learning to recognize each player on a team: some are there to help you win, others could cause you to lose if you don't know how to manage them.

The first major division to understand is between debt that drives you and debt that holds you back. We call debt that drives you good debt, and debt that holds you back bad debt. But let's go a step further and look at the specific types so you know how each one works and what you should keep in mind.

One of the most common types is credit card debt. It's easy to get, affordable for almost everyone, and that's why it's the most dangerous if not used wisely. Credit cards act as borrowed money, given to you upfront. You can buy things without having the money at the time, but you'll have to pay it back later, with interest if you don't do so within the agreed-upon timeframe. The problem is that credit card interest rates are usually sky-high. If you don't pay everything on time, the debt grows very quickly. Credit cards can be useful if you know how to use them, for example, for purchases you know you can pay off quickly. But if you use them as an extension of your paycheck or as if they were free money, you're headed straight for a financial hole.

Then we have personal loans. These are loans you borrow from a bank or other financial institution for any purpose: to pay off a previous debt, cover an emergency, make a large purchase, or even go on a trip. They typically have lower rates than credit cards, but they also vary depending on your credit history. The key with personal loans is to understand how much you'll pay in total. Not just how much they're lending you, but how much you'll end up paying back. This type of debt can be useful if you need to consolidate larger debts or if you really need the money for something important, but you shouldn't borrow it just on impulse or to buy unnecessary things.

Another very common type of debt is student debt. This type of loan is used to pay for university or technical studies, and in many countries it has special conditions, such as lower rates or longer repayment terms. Student debt can be an investment if you choose a career with good job opportunities. You're investing in yourself, in your ability to earn more income in the future. However, it can also become a trap if you study something you don't like, that has no job prospects, or if you don't finish your degree. Taking out student debt requires planning, not just enthusiasm.

Mortgage debt also deserves special mention. This is the debt you acquire when you buy a property. You borrow a large sum of money to buy a house or apartment, and you pay it off over many years. This is typically one of the largest debts a person can have, but it's also one of the most stable if managed well. The property you buy usually increases in value over time, and you're also paying for something that belongs to you. It's a debt that, if you choose it well and can sustain the payments, can be a key step toward your financial freedom.

But it can also turn into a nightmare if you buy more than you can afford or if you don't fully understand the loan terms.

There's also business debt. This type of debt is taken on with the goal of starting or growing a business. It's one of the smartest ways to use debt if you know what you're doing. The idea is to borrow money to invest in something that will generate income: a store, a service company, an online platform, whatever. But it's not for everyone. Starting a business with debt can be a success or a failure. That's why you need a business plan, a good understanding of your market, and a clear idea of how and when you'll repay the money.

Another interesting type is auto debt. Many people buy cars on credit, either with bank loans or direct financing from the dealership. It's important to be careful here. A car loses value from the moment you drive it off the lot, so it's not an investment, but an expense. If you need a car for work, to transport your family, or to make your life easier, it may make sense to go into debt to buy it, as long as the payment doesn't overwhelm you each month. But going into debt for a luxury car just for the sake of appearance or whim is a classic mistake that ruins many pockets.

There are also informal debts, which are those you take on from family, friends, or unregulated lenders. The risk here is not only financial but also emotional. Personal relationships can be damaged when money is involved, especially if the terms are unclear or if repayment problems arise. It's best to avoid this type of debt if you can. And if there's no other option, do it in writing, with clear terms, as if you were with a bank. Sometimes, informality leads to more conflicts than solutions.

Each type of debt has its own rules, risks, and benefits. The important thing is to learn to recognize them, read the contracts, understand the interest rates, terms, and what you're committing to. Not all debt is bad, but all need to be understood before signing anything. Debt can make or break you, but the difference isn't in the type of loan, but in how you use it, why you take it out, and how you plan to repay it.

When you learn to identify each type of debt, you can make smarter decisions. You can say no when necessary and confidently say yes when debt is a tool to achieve something important. Understanding debt is a fundamental part of understanding money. And once you understand it, you no longer fear it. You begin to use it for what it is: a powerful tool that, when used properly, can open many doors for you.

The Good Debt

There's a kind of debt that can change your life for the better. A debt that doesn't drag you down, but pushes you forward. A debt that doesn't take away your freedom, but gives you opportunities. That's good debt. And while many people don't even believe such a thing exists, the reality is that it does, and it can be one of the most powerful tools you can use to build a solid future.

Good debt is debt you use to acquire something that will generate income or increase in value over time. It's debt that leaves you in a better financial position than you were before taking it on. It's not an impulsive expense, an emotional purchase, or a way out of stress. It's a calm, strategic decision aimed at growing your wealth or your ability to earn money.

A clear example of good debt is when you take out a loan to buy a property you'll rent. Imagine you buy a small apartment with a mortgage and then rent it out to someone else. If the rent you receive is equal to or greater than the monthly loan payment, that asset is paying for itself. You're accumulating an asset that, in addition to providing you with income each month, will likely appreciate over time. You're using money that isn't yours to build wealth. That's good debt.

Another typical case is when you go into debt to study for a degree or pursue training that will allow you to increase your income in the future. Maybe you don't have the money to pay for college or a programming course today, but if you access an educational loan and truly take advantage of that training, what you're doing is investing in yourself. And that can give you a much greater return than debt. You're not spending, you're sowing.

It's also good debt when you borrow money to start or expand a profitable business. Of course, this isn't something to be done lightly. It's not about taking out a loan and launching any idea without validating it, hoping it'll magically work. But if you already have a growing business and need capital to buy more inventory, improve your premises, hire staff, or launch a marketing campaign that you know will bring results, then going into debt can be a very smart move. You're

using that money to make more money. That's the heart of good debt.

Good debt has some clear characteristics that you should learn to identify. First, it's backed by a plan. It's not taken on impulse, but with numbers and foresight. You know how much you're going to borrow, how much you're going to pay, and for how long. You're not guessing, you're calculating. Second, it has a clear return. You can clearly see how that debt will generate income or save you money in the future. Third, it's sustainable. It doesn't compromise more than 30 or 40 percent of your monthly income. If debt leaves you with no room to live, it's no longer good, even if the purpose is good.

Many people confuse good debt with big debt. They believe that if they're borrowing a lot of money, it's already an investment. But size doesn't determine whether it's good or bad. What makes it good is that it works for you. That it generates a positive flow. That the borrowed money produces more than it costs. Sometimes, a small debt, well used, can give you more benefits than a huge, poorly planned debt.

Now, we shouldn't idealize good debt as if it were magic. There's no such thing as risk-free debt. All debt involves commitment and all requires responsibility. Even the best investment can go wrong if the market changes or if you make mistakes in your calculations. That's why it's so important to prepare, study, and not make financial decisions based solely on optimism or because someone else did. Good debt requires you to be calm, strategic, and consistent.

Another advantage of good debt is that it improves your credit history if you pay it off properly. Every time you take on debt and manage it well, banks and institutions see that you're a trustworthy person. And that opens the door to better terms in the future. You can access larger loans, with lower interest rates and greater flexibility. It's like building your financial reputation. The better you build it, the more resources you'll have to grow.

One of the biggest differences between people who are financially advancing and those who are stagnant is how they use debt. While some see it as a curse, others understand it as a tool. And like any tool, you have to learn how to use it. A hammer can help you build a house or it can break a window. It's not the hammer. It's how you use it.

When you begin to view debt as a tool for generating wealth, your relationship with money changes. You begin to think about opportunities, investments, and profitability. You stop mindless consumption and begin making purposeful decisions. And when you do that, not only does your bank account grow. So does your security, your confidence, and your ability to build a life with greater freedom.

Good debt isn't something everyone uses, but it's within reach of anyone who decides to learn. You don't need to be rich to use it. You need to be smart. And be willing to plan, learn, and act consciously. If you do that, debt ceases to be an obstacle and becomes an ally. A powerful, useful, and very effective one.

Bad Debt

Bad debt is like that friend who seems nice at first, invites you out, makes you feel good for a moment, but always ends up getting you into trouble. It's easy to accept, tempting, and usually comes with promises that sound perfect: "buy now, pay later," "interest-free installments," "pre-approved credit," "you don't need any cash to get what you want." Everything sounds good until it's time to pay, and that's when the disaster begins. Bad debt doesn't give you anything worth more than what you're paying. It doesn't make you grow, it doesn't give you income, it just leaves you with an outstanding bill and less freedom.

This debt arises when you buy things you don't need, with money you don't have, to impress people you don't even care about. It's the debt you use to consume instead of invest. It's the debt you pay in endless installments for a new cell phone, a designer outfit, or a vacation you really couldn't afford. At the time, it seems harmless. The payment is low, they approve it in minutes, and they even make you feel special for giving you access to that credit. But as the months go by, you realize you're paying much more than the product was worth, and that each month your money disappears as soon as it arrives.

One of the most common examples of bad debt is irresponsible credit card use. When you don't pay your balance in full each month, the interest begins to accumulate, and the debt snowballs downhill. Credit cards have some of the highest interest rates on the market, and if you only pay the minimum, you can spend years paying off your debt without really reducing it. The worst part is that you often don't even remember what you spent it on. It was meals, outings, a gift, maybe an emotional purchase. Nothing that's generating value in your life now.

Bad debt also arises when you take out personal loans just to cover recurring financial gaps. If you need to borrow every month to make ends meet, something is wrong with your financial structure. And if you do it to cover another old debt, you enter a dangerous cycle. It's like opening one gap to cover another. At some point, you won't have the means to cover the next one, and that's when the real anguish begins.

Another typical case is going into debt to buy a luxury car when your finances don't allow it. Sometimes we think we need something expensive to demonstrate success, but if the car represents more than 20 or 30 percent of your monthly income, and you financed it with a long-term loan, you're putting a noose around your neck. A car loses value over time, doesn't generate income, and has additional expenses such as fuel, maintenance, and insurance. Going into debt to buy one is more of an emotional decision than a financial one, and it often ends up being a burden.

Bad debt is silent. You don't always realize you're falling into it. Sometimes it starts with a single purchase, a poorly managed emergency, an impulse. But then it becomes a habit. And suddenly you find yourself living on the edge, with no room to save, no ability to invest, no peace of mind. You're constantly thinking about the next payment, how to stretch your money, what you're going to skip this month. That's not freedom. That's financial slavery.

And the saddest thing is that many people feel trapped in that situation. They believe they can't get out, that bad debt is part of adulthood. But that's not the case. You can always correct your course. First, by understanding what got you there. Was it an unnecessary purchase? A lack of planning? An unsupported medical emergency? Then, by taking responsibility. Stop blaming the bank, the system, or society. Most of the time, we're the ones who said yes. And if we made the decision to go into debt, we can also make the decision to get out.

Bad debt is fought with awareness. Before borrowing, ask yourself simple questions: Will this generate income? Will this be useful to me in five years? Am I buying out of necessity or impulse? Could I wait and save for this instead of paying it off with interest? These questions may seem basic, but they make all the difference. Because when you get used to thinking before you go into debt, you begin to regain control.

And something very important: getting out of bad debt isn't just a financial issue, it's also an emotional one. We often use spending to fill voids, to calm anxiety, to feel like we're moving forward, even if it's just for a few hours. But that relief is fleeting. What's left afterward is the bill. That's why real change begins when you decide to take care of your mind as much as your wallet. When you understand that you don't need to impress anyone, that you don't need to have everything now, and that freedom is worth more than anything bought with debt.

Bad debt doesn't look the same to everyone. What's unnecessary for one person may be a necessity for another. But there's one principle that never fails: if what you buy with debt doesn't give you more than it costs, it probably wasn't worth going into debt. The challenge is having the courage to wait, to say no, to plan. Because yes, it's much easier to pull out the credit card and resolve it right away. But it's much smarter to wait, save, and buy with your own money. That's the difference between living in debt and living in peace.

The goal isn't to live debt-free forever, but to learn how to use it well. And that starts with stopping the traps of bad debt. You don't need more stuff. You need more awareness. More control. More intention. Because when you stop using credit to live a lifestyle you can't sustain, true wealth begins. And that, in the end, is worth far more than anything money can buy.

The Cost of Debt

When most people think about going into debt, they only focus on one thing: how much they'll pay each month. If the monthly payment fits within their budget, they think everything's fine. But what many don't see, or prefer to ignore, is the true cost of debt. Because going into debt isn't simply borrowing money and paying it back in installments. It's much more than that. It's compromising your future, paying a price that's often not noticeable at first but weighs heavily on you over time. And that price, if not properly understood, can end up being very high.

The cost of debt isn't just the amount you borrow. It also includes interest, fees, mandatory insurance, penalties if you're late, and something more invisible but very real: your peace of mind. For example, if you borrow ten thousand dollars at 30 percent annual interest to be paid over five years, you're not just paying back ten thousand dollars. You're paying back much more. In some cases, you may even end up paying double or more than the original amount. This means that the product, investment, or expense you made is costing you much more than it seemed.

Many people are surprised when they see the total they'll end up paying for long-term debt. Of course, the ads only show you the attractiveness: pay in installments, buy now, no cash required. But when they hand you the contract and you do the math, you realize that that TV that cost a thousand, with interest and 24-month installments, is actually going to cost you fifteen hundred or more. And was it worth paying that extra just to get it sooner? Often not. But by then, you've already signed.

One of the most common mistakes is focusing only on the monthly payment without considering the total interest you're paying. A low payment doesn't always mean a good deal. You could be paying for much longer, and in the end, the total cost could be exaggerated. That's why it's so important to always look at the Total Financial Cost, not just what you pay month to month. The bank or finance company isn't doing you a favor. They're doing you a business. And you're the customer. If you don't fully understand how it works, you could end up being the customer who pays the most and receives the least.

In addition to money, debt has another cost: your freedom. Every time you take on debt, you're committing part of your future income. That money you haven't yet earned already has an owner. It's already allocated. That means you'll have less room to save, less capacity to invest, and fewer opportunities to take advantage of opportunities that arise. In other words, less freedom. Because working to live is one thing, and working to pay off debt is quite another. And the sad thing is that many people live like this, chained to their payments, month after month, year after year, unable to make progress.

There's also the emotional toll. This isn't talked about much, but it's real. Living in debt creates stress, anxiety, and worry. It keeps you up at night. It makes you feel like you're always chasing money. That you can't stop. That if something goes wrong, if you lose your job, if you get sick, or if an emergency arises, you won't be able to make ends meet. And that kind of constant pressure affects your health, your relationships, and your productivity. It's not just a matter of numbers. It's an emotional burden that, over time, takes its toll.

That's why it's so important to be mindful before going into debt. Not because debt is inherently bad, but because it comes at a cost. And that cost must be justified. If you're going to go into debt, let it be for something that brings you real value. That helps you grow. That leaves you better off than before. Not on a whim, not because of social pressure, not on impulse. Because every debt you take on is a decision that will affect your life for months or even years. And often that impact is much greater than you imagined.

There's a simple rule that can help you: if you can't pay for something in cash, and it's not something that will generate income or increase in value, you probably shouldn't go into debt for it. Wait. Save. Plan. Because paying interest on something that depreciates or loses value quickly is like throwing money away. And the worst part is that many people do it frequently, without stopping to think about the consequences.

Imagine that for every debt you take on, you're signing a contract that says, "I'm going to work more, I'm going to have less peace of mind, I'm going to postpone my goals—all for this thing I want now." If you think about it this way, maybe you'll start to see things differently. Maybe you'll pause before swiping your card or signing a loan. Maybe you'll start to wonder if the full price of what seems so urgent today is worth it.

And there's another hidden cost to debt, one that almost no one mentions: the opportunity cost. Every peso you pay in interest is a peso you can't use to invest, to save, to create something new. That money, if it weren't tied up in debt, could be working for you. It could be generating more money, giving you more security, bringing you closer to your dreams. But instead, it's spent on monthly payments that only benefit the lender.

Understanding the true cost of debt is one of the most important keys to healthy personal finances. It's not about being afraid of going into debt. It's about doing so with your eyes wide open. With information. With strategy. Because debt can help you or destroy you, depending on how you use it. And that's up to you.

If you learn to look beyond the monthly payment, if you get used to calculating the total cost and asking yourself if it's really worth it, you'll make better decisions. You'll avoid unnecessary debt. You'll have more control over your money. And, most importantly, you'll live with less stress and more freedom. Because in the end, the true cost of debt isn't measured just in money, it's measured in quality of life. And that, believe me, is priceless.

Smart Credit

Using credit wisely is like holding a powerful tool in your hands. If you use it well, you can build something great. If you use it poorly, you can hurt yourself. Credit isn't your enemy, but it's not your automatic salvation either. It's a tool, and like any tool, its value depends on the skill with which you use it. That's why it's so important to understand how it works and, above all, how to get the most out of it without it becoming a burden.

Smart credit starts with a clear mindset: using other people's money to create value, not to satisfy impulsive desires. It's not about going into debt because you want something, but because you need something that will help you be better off tomorrow. Well-used credit can open doors that would otherwise be closed. It can help you study, start a business, grow, and invest. The problem is that many people use it as a way to live beyond their means, and that's where credit stops being smart and becomes a trap.

One of the smartest ways to use credit is to finance assets. What is an asset? Something that puts money in your pocket. If you take out a loan to buy a machine that you'll use in your business and that will generate income every month, that's smart credit. If you buy a property that you'll then rent out, and that rent covers the loan payment and even leaves you with a profit, you're also using credit wisely. You're using someone else's money to make money. That's the basic principle of smart credit.

Another good way to use credit is to acquire education or training that increases your earning capacity. A course, a certification, a degree that will allow you to have a better job or start your own business. Of course, this only works if you truly take advantage of that training and if it has job prospects or practical applications. It's not about studying for the sake of studying, but rather investing in yourself with a clear purpose. If you know that investment will give you more income in the future, then credit makes sense.

Credit can also be smart when it helps you maintain or improve your credit history. For example, using a credit card to make purchases you had already planned, and then paying the total each month interest-free, helps you build a good financial reputation. That reputation can help you later if you want to access a larger loan, such as a mortgage to buy a house. But be careful, this only works if you're very disciplined. If you fall behind or only pay the minimum, credit is no longer your ally.

A key aspect of smart credit is having a payment plan before going into debt. Never take out a loan without knowing exactly how you're going to pay it. Don't wait until the first installment arrives to think about how you'll get by. Before signing any contract or swiping a card, do the math. Ask yourself: Can I comfortably pay this each month without affecting the essentials of my life? What would happen if I lost my income for a while? Do I have an emergency fund? Thinking about this before going into debt is what makes the difference between smart use and impulsive use.

Smart credit also involves comparing options. Don't accept the first loan offered to you. Compare interest rates, terms, fees, and conditions. Sometimes the difference between one loan and another may seem small, but over time it can add up to a lot of money. Get informed. Ask questions. Don't be afraid to negotiate. Sometimes just asking can get you better terms. And remember that not all loans are the same. There are personal loans, mortgage loans, consumer loans, student loans, and business loans. Each has its advantages and risks. Knowing them empowers you.

A very common mistake is using credit to solve temporary problems without addressing the underlying cause. For example, taking out a loan to pay off old debts or to make ends meet when your income isn't enough. This may give you momentary relief, but if you don't address the root of the problem, you're just kicking the can down the road. Smart credit doesn't fill gaps; it builds solutions. If you use it to stay afloat, sooner or later you'll sink. But if you use it to move forward, it can propel you far.

It's also important to consider the impact of credit on your monthly cash flow. Don't go into debt beyond your ability to pay. A good rule of thumb is to keep your total payments to no more than 30 percent of your income. If you go over that, you'll start to feel pressure. And if you fall behind, you not only pay more in interest and penalties, but you also damage your credit history. A bad credit history closes doors, charges you higher rates, and leaves you with fewer options when you really need them.

Smart credit is cold, unemotional. It's not driven by whims, trends, or comparing yourself to others. It's driven by logic, calculation, and strategy. If something doesn't make financial sense, it's not worth going into debt for. It doesn't matter how many times you see it on social media, or how many people share it. Financial intelligence doesn't seek to impress anyone. It seeks freedom, peace of mind, and growth. And that is built step by step, with conscious and well-thought-out decisions.

Ultimately, well-managed credit can be a springboard to a fuller, more stable, and freer life. But it requires responsibility. Because even if the money isn't yours, the commitment is. And if you fulfill that commitment strategically, your credit becomes a lever of power. It's not a matter of avoiding credit at all costs, but rather of understanding it and using it to your advantage. As a powerful tool that, when used properly, can help you build the life you dream of, without sacrificing your peace of mind along the way.

Building Your Credit History

Building a credit history is like planting a seed that will bear fruit over time. It's not a magical or instant process, but rather a series of daily actions that help you build a solid and reliable financial reputation. It all starts with small decisions, like paying your bills on time and not exceeding your credit limits. Every time you meet your commitments, you send a positive message to financial institutions, showing that you are responsible and that they can trust you when they need support.

To begin, it's important to understand that your credit history is a record of how you handle borrowed money. It's similar to a resume, where every action counts. Paying on time is the foundation of everything. While it may be tempting to miss a small fee or postpone a payment, every delay negatively impacts this history. Credit bureaus record every detail, and in the long run, those small oversights can add up and take away your opportunities. Therefore, it's essential to be punctual and organize your finances so you never find yourself in trouble.

Another key aspect is the moderate and conscious use of credit cards. Cards are a very useful tool for building credit history, as long as they are used wisely. It's preferable to use them for planned purchases that you know you'll be able to pay off immediately, rather than resorting to them in moments of desperation or to purchase goods you don't really need. With each on-time payment, you improve your credit score, which translates into future benefits, such as lower interest rates and greater access to credit on favorable terms. It's a virtuous cycle: the better you take care of your credit history, the more opportunities you'll have to grow financially.

Furthermore, it's vital to diversify the types of credit you use. It's not about having an overwhelming number of cards or loans, but rather demonstrating that you can manage different types of obligations. Perhaps you have an auto loan, a personal loan, or even a mortgage. Each of these credits, when managed correctly, adds a positive aspect to your credit history. However, it's crucial that you keep your debts within reasonable limits. Excessive credit use can be seen as a sign of risk by lenders, and that will negatively affect your financial reputation. The important thing is to find the right balance that allows you to demonstrate responsibility without overburdening yourself.

Building a healthy credit history also involves knowing the tools and resources available to you. There are online services that allow you to review your credit report, identify errors, and monitor your progress. Review these reports periodically to ensure all the information is accurate. Sometimes, administrative errors can harm your credit history through no fault of your own. If you detect any inconsistencies, contact the appropriate institution immediately. This demonstrates not only your commitment to your obligations but also your interest in keeping everything in order, which translates into greater trust from financial institutions.

Patience is another fundamental element in this process. Building a solid credit history takes time and, above all, discipline. Don't expect results overnight. Every on-time payment, every well-thought-out purchase, and every effort to maintain control of your spending are steps that, when combined, will allow you to achieve financial freedom. It's a path that, although it may seem long at first, will open doors for you in the future. When you need credit to buy a home, start a business, or invest in your education, you'll have an impeccable credit history to support your application and offer you better financing terms.

Don't forget that your credit history also speaks to your character. It's a reflection of your commitment, your organization, and your ability to plan for the future. Every on-time payment, every successful transaction, is a testament to your discipline. And that discipline not only opens doors for you in the financial world, but also teaches you to value the importance of responsibility in all aspects of life. Thus, by building and maintaining your credit history, you become a trustworthy person, both to yourself and to the world around you.

Finally, it's good to remember that a good credit history doesn't mean you should go into excessive debt. Rather, it's about using credit consciously and strategically. It's not about seeking credit just for the sake of it, but rather using it as a tool that, when managed well, allows you to achieve important goals. This approach will help you avoid common mistakes and consolidate a financial foundation that will last a lifetime. With discipline, planning, and time, you'll see that every effort is worth it and that, little by little, your financial reputation will become one of your greatest strengths.

How to Use Credit Cards Without Being Used by Them

Credit cards are like sharp knives. In experienced hands, they're good for preparing a great meal. In inexperienced hands, they can end up causing an accident. The problem isn't the card itself, but how you use it. Many people fall into the trap of thinking the card is an extension of their money, as if they have more income just because the bank approved them for a loan. But the truth is, everything you spend on a credit card has to be paid back, with interest, if you don't do it on time. And those interest rates aren't low. They're high, often sky-high. So if you don't understand how a credit card works, you can end up being used by it, instead of using it to your advantage.

The first rule for using a credit card wisely is very simple: never spend more than you can afford to pay off in a single month. If you buy something with the card, make sure you have the money in your account to pay for it when the due date arrives. Don't view the card as a way to finance your life, but rather as a tool to stay organized, take advantage of benefits, or build your credit history. If you buy something expensive and leave it financed for several months, paying only the minimum, you'll end up paying double or even triple what it originally cost. That's letting the card use you.

Using the monthly lump sum payment is the best-kept secret in the financial world. If you use your card and pay 100 percent of your balance by the due date, you pay zero interest. And at the same time, you're accumulating points, miles, cashback, or any other benefit your card offers. That's how you play it smart. But the moment you decide to pay only the minimum or leave part of your balance for later, the bank starts charging you interest. And that interest adds up fast. What seemed like a small expense snowballs into a bigger amount every month.

Another important point is to understand your cut-off date and your payment date. The cut-off date is the day the bank reviews everything you spent during the last payment cycle. From there, it gives you a deadline to pay. Many people make the mistake of using their card without knowing when it's best for them. If you make a purchase right after the cut-off date, you gain almost a full month before you have to pay it off. But if you make it right before, you'll have to pay within a few days. Knowing this detail allows you to better organize your purchases and have more time to prepare your payment.

The credit limit your bank gives you isn't a goal you should reach. It's just a ceiling. It doesn't mean you should spend everything you're allowed. In fact, if you're always close to the limit, your credit score can be negatively affected. Ideally, you should use less than 30 percent of your limit, and if you can use less than 10 percent, even better. This shows financial institutions that you're a responsible person and that you don't rely entirely on credit. The lower your utilization, the healthier your financial profile looks.

You also need to be careful with cash advances. Although your card allows you to withdraw money from an ATM, this is one of the most expensive ways to use it. From the moment you make an advance, you start charging interest, with no grace period. Plus, you're often charged an additional fee just for withdrawing the money. Unless it's an extreme emergency, avoid this option. There are better ways to resolve a financial emergency than resorting to a cash advance on a card.

Another important tip is to understand the fees and costs associated with your card. Some cards have fees for annual maintenance, international purchases, currency exchange, over-limit fees, late payments, and more. Read the contract, review your statement, and make sure you understand all the terms and conditions. Many people don't realize they're overpaying simply because they didn't pay attention. And the worst part is that some of these fees are avoidable if you use your card wisely.

The card can also be your ally if you know how to take advantage of its benefits. Some offer discounts in stores, promotions, points you can redeem for products or travel, travel insurance, extended warranties, and more. But these benefits are only worth it if you don't charge interest for using them. If you end up paying more in interest than you save with the benefits, you're not earning anything. So the first thing is to use the card healthily, and then take advantage of the extras it offers.

Something else worth mentioning is that you don't need a lot of cards. One or two well-managed cards are enough to build a good credit history and access benefits. Having too many cards can cause you to lose track of your spending, forget payments, and end up creating unnecessary complications. More cards doesn't mean more wealth or more power. It means more responsibility and more risk if you don't manage them well. Focus on thoroughly understanding the ones you have and use them strategically.

Finally, remember that credit cards aren't a lifeline. They're not there to bail you out when you're in financial trouble. If you're going through a tough time financially, credit cards may seem like a quick fix, but in reality, you're just postponing the problem. The best thing to do in these cases is to review your budget, adjust your spending, look for additional income, and build an emergency fund for the future. Credit should be used to grow, not to fill gaps.

When you learn to use a credit card wisely, it stops being a threat and becomes a valuable tool. But that requires discipline, knowledge, and control. It's not difficult, but it does require attention. Don't get carried away by the excitement of spending or the illusion of having more money. Use the card for what it is: a means to achieve your goals, not an excuse to live beyond your means. If you control it, it can help you achieve many things. But if you let it control you, sooner or later, it will take its toll. And it won't be cheap.

Financial Planning with Debt

Many people believe that having debt means you can't plan your finances. As if it were an obstacle that leaves you out of the financial game. But in reality, financial planning is even more important when you have debt. Because if you don't have a plan, your debts control you. But if you make a clear plan, you take control. Having debt doesn't prevent you from moving forward; what stops you is not knowing how to manage what you owe. Therefore, this chapter is an invitation to stop fearing debt and start organizing it intelligently, with a clear, step-by-step strategy.

The first thing is to get a complete picture of your situation. Many people don't know exactly how much they owe. They have debts in different places, with different amounts, interest rates, and payment dates. And because they don't have everything clear, it feels like a dark cloud hanging over their heads. But once you put it all out in the open, things don't seem so scary anymore. Make a detailed list of all your debts: how much you owe, to whom, what the interest rate is, what the minimum payment is, and when the due date is. Without that, it's impossible to make a plan. That list is your starting point.

The next step is to analyze your cash flow. How much do you earn each month? What are your fixed and variable expenses? Where is your money going? This is where many people are surprised. They discover they spend much more than they thought on small things: eating out, subscriptions they don't use, impulse purchases. Identifying these leaks is key. Because to effectively pay off your debt, you need to free up money. And to free it up, you need to know where it's going. It's not about living a miserable life, but about making small adjustments that allow you more room to meet your commitments.

Once you know what you owe and how much money you actually have available, you can establish a payment strategy. You have several options here. One is the snowball method. It involves ordering your debts from smallest to largest, regardless of interest, and paying off the smallest first while maintaining the minimum payments on the others. When the smallest one disappears, you take that money and use it to pay off the next one, and so on. This method is very useful because it gives you quick motivation: seeing one debt decrease gives you the impetus to continue.

Another method is the avalanche method. In this case, you order your debts by interest rate, from highest to lowest. You start with the most expensive, the one that charges you the most interest. Even if it takes longer to see results, you'll actually save more money in the long run. This method is mathematically more efficient, but it can be emotionally more difficult if you don't see quick progress. There's no single right way. The important thing is to choose the one that works best for you and stick with it.

While you're working on paying off your debt, it's also critical to avoid new ones. Many people take one step forward by paying off one debt, only to take two steps back by going into debt again. This is especially common with credit cards. The temptation is there, just a click or a swipe away. That's why it's key to plan your monthly spending and stick to a realistic budget. If something isn't in the budget, you don't buy it. It's that simple. Planning with debt means being more disciplined, more aware, and more committed to yourself.

One aspect that not many people consider in their planning is their emergency fund. You might think there's no point in saving if you're in debt, but it's the opposite. Having a small emergency fund, even if it's just a few hundred dollars, can prevent you from going back into debt if something unexpected arises. A doctor's visit, a car repair, or an unexpected bill shouldn't push you deeper into debt. So, while you're paying off your debt, try to set aside a small portion, even if it's symbolic, into that fund. Over time, it will become your safety net.

Another key step in your financial planning with debt is setting clear goals. What do you want to achieve in the next six months? In a year? In five? Not all goals have to be huge. It can be something like paying off a credit card completely, cutting your debt level in half, or simply stopping using credit for everyday expenses. Goals give you direction. They help you make smarter decisions.

Because when you know where you're going, it's easier to say no to things that aren't good for you.

Renegotiating your debts is also very helpful if you feel trapped. Many people believe that the terms of a loan or credit card are set in stone, but that's not the case. You can call your bank or creditor and ask for better terms. In some cases, you can get a lower rate, a longer payment plan, or even a reduction in your total debt. It won't always work, but it's worth a try. Showing your willingness to pay already puts you in a better position. And if you manage to reduce your interest, that can greatly accelerate your progress.

Planning also includes constantly reviewing your progress. Don't make a plan and then forget it. Every month, review how you're doing. Did you pay what you planned? Did unexpected expenses change your numbers? Can you make any adjustments? Financial planning with debt isn't a one-and-done thing. It's a living process. It changes with you. It evolves with your income, your decisions, and your circumstances. But if you keep it active, if you adjust it, and follow it with discipline, it will give you concrete results.

And finally, there's something you can't buy or plan on a spreadsheet, but it's just as important: your attitude. Having a good relationship with money, letting go of the guilt of having debt, and accepting your situation with maturity is an essential part of the process. It's not about living in fear or hiding from your bank statements. It's about facing it calmly, with clarity, and with action. Because when you have a plan, debt stops being an invisible monster and becomes a challenge you can manage.

In short, financial planning with debt isn't a luxury; it's a necessity. It's the bridge between where you are now and where you want to be. It doesn't matter how large your debt is. The important thing is that you stop, face it head-on, and build a path out. With order, patience, and intelligence. Because debt doesn't disappear on its own, but it can stop being a burden if you decide to act. Planning is deciding to take the helm of your ship and steer it toward a better destination. And if you do, no debt can defeat you.

Refinance or Restructure

When you're stuck in debt that feels like a dead end, there are two words that can offer you a new opportunity: refinancing and restructuring. They sound technical, almost like something only banks understand, but they're actually tools available to anyone who wants to take control of their financial situation. And if you use them well, they can be like a breath of fresh air when you feel like you're up to your neck in water. The problem is that many people don't even know these options exist or, worse yet, believe that asking for them is a sign of failure. But it's quite the opposite: asking for them is a sign of financial intelligence.

First, let's understand what refinancing means. Refinancing a debt is basically changing the conditions under which you're paying what you owe. It's like being offered a second chance to start over with new rules. For example, if you have a personal loan with a high interest rate, you can approach your bank or another lender and ask for a new loan to pay off the old one, but with a lower rate. By doing so, you reduce the amount of interest you'll pay over the long term and therefore lighten your monthly burden.

Sometimes you can also extend the term of the loan, which lowers the amount you pay each month, even though you'll end up paying more interest overall. The idea here is to give yourself a breathing space so you can reorganize your finances without feeling suffocated.

Now, restructuring is different, although it has a similar objective. Restructuring doesn't mean changing your debt, but rather directly renegotiating the debt you already have. It's like sitting down with your creditor and saying, "Look, the terms we agreed to no longer work for me. Can we make a new agreement that allows me to continue paying without going under?" In this process, you can achieve a reduction in the monthly payment, an extension of the term, a pause in payments, or even a reduction in the total amount you owe if the creditor agrees. Many financial institutions prefer to negotiate with you rather than take your case to a collection agency or lose all their money. But for this to work, you have to show a real willingness to pay. They have to see that you're not running away, but rather seeking a solution.

And how do you know if you should refinance or restructure? The key lies in your current situation. If your debt is up to date, but your monthly payments are too high or you're paying exorbitant interest rates, then refinancing may be your best option. This allows you to seek better terms without having to default. On the other hand, if you're already behind, if you haven't been able to pay for several months, and the collection calls have already started, then restructuring is probably what you need. In that case, it's no longer about avoiding the problem, but about directly addressing it with the lender.

Many banks and lenders have refinancing and restructuring programs. The problem is, they don't always advertise them. They won't call you to offer help if you don't ask for it. You have to be the one to take the first step. And when you do, it's important to do so with preparation. Before applying for refinancing, research other options. Compare rates. See if another bank can offer you better terms to settle your current debt. Sometimes, switching banks can mean big savings. But be sure to read the fine print.

Don't be tempted by a lower payment if the interest rates are worse. And if you're going to restructure, be prepared to negotiate clearly. Bring your numbers. Prove you can pay if they give you better terms.

It's also important to consider the associated costs. Refinancing may involve fees, new insurance, or administrative costs. Restructuring may also involve late fees or penalties, although these are often waived during the negotiation. That's why it's key to do the math. To compare the before and after. To see not only how much you'll pay each month, but also how much you'll pay in total. And to make a decision based on what's really best for you, not just what seems easiest at the moment.

Some people refinance or restructure and feel liberated. But others, as soon as they feel that relief, go back into debt. It's like digging themselves out of a hole. That's what you must avoid at all costs. If you decide to use these tools, do so as part of a larger strategy. A strategy that includes a budget, an emergency fund, and a firm commitment to not fall back into the same habits that got you into trouble. It's not just about fixing your debt, but about transforming your relationship with money.

Refinancing or restructuring isn't cheating or giving up. It's playing your cards right. It's admitting you need to change something and taking action before it's too late. It's giving yourself permission to improve your situation without carrying the shame of having made mistakes. We all make financial mistakes. What makes the difference is what you do afterward. So if you feel like debt is overwhelming you, don't see it as the end. See it as an opportunity to reorganize, to negotiate, and to start a new chapter. One where you take control, one where your decisions bring you closer to the financial freedom you deserve.

Debt to Invest

There's an idea that might sound a little crazy if you haven't heard it before: borrowing to invest. For many people, the word debt alone causes fear, stress, and mistrust. And if you add the word "invest" to that, it seems like a recipe for disaster. But if you understand it well and do it intelligently, borrowing to invest can be one of the most profitable decisions of your life. The trick is knowing how, when, and why to do it. Because it's not about going into debt on a whim or out of emotion, but with strategy, with cold numbers, and a growth mindset.

Investable debt is one of the clearest forms of what we call good debt. It's the kind of debt that gives you more than it takes away. Instead of being a burden, it becomes a tool that helps you generate income. The idea is simple: you borrow money to put it to work, and that money produces enough profit to pay off the debt and leave you with something extra. In other words, you not only repay what you borrowed, but you also generate a profit. Sounds good, right? But for it to work, you have to do it wisely.

Let's consider a simple example. Imagine you see an opportunity to buy a property that costs $100,000. You don't have all the money, but you can take out a mortgage loan. You pay a down payment, say $20,000, and the bank lends you the other $80,000. You buy the property, fix it up a bit, and rent it out. Each month, the tenant pays you rent that covers the loan payment and leaves you with something extra. Or maybe you decide to sell the property after a while and make a profit. In that case, you used the bank's money to build wealth. That's using debt to invest wisely.

You can also use debt to invest in a business. Suppose you have a clear idea, a solid plan, and know how to generate income with a startup. But you lack the initial capital. You can turn to a business loan or line of credit to get your business off the ground. Of course, this isn't something you should just wing. If you lack experience, haven't done your research, or are acting on impulse, you can end up losing money and getting stuck in debt. But if you do your homework, understand your market, and know how to manage the risks, borrowing to start a business can change your life.

Another common type of debt investment is that used to invest in education. Although this may not seem like a direct financial investment, it is. Studying for a university degree, a specialization, a technical course, or any type of training that will allow you to earn more money in the future is also an investment. If the debt you take on for education translates into higher income in the following years, then it was good debt. The problem comes when people go into debt to study something that isn't in demand, that they don't enjoy, or that simply doesn't provide a return. That's when it becomes useless debt. Therefore, even education as an investment must be considered strategically.

Now, not everything that seems like an investment really is. Many people deceive themselves. For example, taking out a loan to buy a car you use to commute isn't, in and of itself, an investment. It's a necessary expense, yes, but it doesn't generate income. On the other hand, if you use that same car to work as a driver, make deliveries, or any activity that directly generates money, then it can be considered an investment. The key is this: if the debt produces cash flow into your pocket, then it makes sense. If the money just goes out and doesn't come back, then it's a disguised expense.

But be careful. Using debt to invest has its risks. Like any investment, it can go wrong. Maybe the business doesn't work out, the property isn't rented out, or the investment doesn't yield the expected returns. That's why, before taking out debt to invest, you need to do the math with brutal honesty. How much will the debt cost you? How much could you earn from the investment? What happens if things don't go as expected? Do you have a Plan B? Do you have an emergency fund? Do you know what you're doing, or are you just acting on blind faith? It's not about being afraid, but about being clear. Fear paralyzes, but clarity protects you.

It's also essential to understand the terms of the loan. Not all loans are created equal. Some have very high rates that can eat into your profits. Others have very short terms that don't give you time to recoup your investment. Therefore, before signing any document, make sure you read it carefully, understand what you're agreeing to, and compare different options. A poorly negotiated loan can ruin a good investment. And a well-negotiated one can multiply your results.

In short, going into debt to invest can be a great decision if you do it strategically, with analysis, and a long-term vision. It's not for amateurs or dreamers without a plan. It's for people who are willing to learn, calculate, and take risks responsibly. It's a powerful tool, but like any tool, if you use it incorrectly, it can hurt you. But if you use it well, it can be the first step toward a much more prosperous life, where money works for you and not the other way around. Debt, in this case, ceases to be a burden and becomes a lever. And with the right lever, you can move the world.

Common Debt Mistakes and How to Avoid Them

One of the biggest problems with debt isn't the debt itself, but the mistakes we make when using it. Most people don't learn about money management in school, let alone how to handle debt properly. Because of this, they fall into common traps that end up costing them years of their lives and thousands of dollars out of their pockets. But the good news is that these mistakes aren't impossible mysteries to understand. In fact, once you know them, you can easily avoid them. And if you've already fallen into one, it's also possible to get out of it with strategy, not guilt.

The first mistake, and perhaps the most common, is going into impulse debt. It happens when you buy something just because you want it at the moment, without giving it much thought, and you use a credit card or take out a loan without a plan to repay it. It's what happens when you go to the mall, see something you like, and think, "I'll pay for it later." But that "later" turns into months, interest, and stress. Impulse is the enemy of healthy finances. If you can't pay for it in cash, at least make sure it's not an emotional purchase. Wait a day. Ask yourself if you really need it. If after thinking about it, it's still worth it, then consider it calmly, not in a hurry.

Another very common mistake is paying only the minimum on your credit card. This may seem harmless, but it's a dangerous trap. Credit card companies make a lot of money when you do this, because the interest keeps accruing and the principal barely decreases. You can spend years paying off a small debt just by paying no more than the minimum. The best way to use a credit card is to pay it off in full before the due date. If you can't do that, at least pay much more than the minimum. If you only make the minimum payment, the debt traps you and snowballs into something that grows over time.

A third mistake is not knowing exactly how much you owe. Some people have three, four, or more credit cards, a personal loan, a car loan, and even an informal debt with a friend. And the most alarming thing is that they lack control. They don't know how much they owe in total, how much they're paying in interest, or when payments are due. Lack of clarity is the enemy of financial control. If you don't know how much you owe, you can't make a real plan to get out of that situation. The first step is always to lay everything out on the table. Write down each debt, with its amount, interest, monthly payment, and due date. Only with this information can you make smart decisions.

It's also a very common mistake to take out loans to pay off other loans without improving the terms. This is called "kicking the debt." You do this when, for example, you use one credit card to pay off another, or take out a loan with the same rate just to cover the payment on another. All you're doing is moving the problem, not solving it. If you're going to consolidate your debts, it has to be with a better rate, a better term, or a clear repayment strategy. Otherwise, you're just prolonging your pain and postponing collapse.

Another serious mistake is using debt for show. It's when you buy things you can't afford just to show off an image of success that isn't real. This happens a lot with expensive clothes, the latest cell phones, new cars, or vacations paid for on credit. The problem isn't indulging yourself once in a while; the problem is building a fictitious life financed with money you don't have. And the worst part is that social media has intensified this problem. Many people go into debt to look good in front of others, even if they're filled with anxiety inside. True financial success isn't what you see, it's what you feel. It's the peace of mind that comes from knowing you're not stuck in endless payments for things you didn't need.

It's also very dangerous to ignore loan terms. Many people sign contracts without reading or understanding them. They only look at the monthly payment, but not at the interest rate, the total term, or any late fees. This leads to unpleasant surprises, such as hidden fees or unexpected increases in the monthly payment. Always read everything. And if you don't understand, ask. It's better to appear insistent than to end up trapped for not having read an important clause.

Another mistake that causes many problems is not having an emergency fund. People get into debt because they don't have savings. All they have to do is break down their car, get sick, or lose their job, and the first thing they do is take out their credit card or take out a loan. But if you had a small cushion of money saved, you could avoid a lot of unnecessary debt. An emergency fund is like a shield. It's not for vacations or shopping sprees; it's to protect you from the unexpected. If you don't have one, start small. Ten, twenty, or fifty dollars a month. The important thing is to start.

And finally, one of the most serious mistakes: giving up. Some people, feeling deeply in debt, simply disconnect. They stop answering calls, ignore emails, throw away unopened bank statements. Instead of looking for solutions, they paralyze themselves. And that only makes everything worse. Debt, like any problem, doesn't go away if you ignore it. It grows bigger. But if you face it, even step by step, you can control it. You can negotiate, you can reorganize, you can move forward. Giving up is never the answer. Learning is the way.

In conclusion, debt isn't the problem; debt mistakes are. And the good news is that all of these mistakes can be avoided with education, attention, and small, conscious decisions. You don't need to be a financial expert to manage your debt intelligently. You just need to be present, think before you act, and remember that every decision counts. If you're in a difficult situation today, you're not alone. But you're not doomed either. You can get out. You can learn. And you can build a much freer and happier financial life, free from the mistakes that held you back in the past.

Debt and Emotions

Talking about debt isn't just about numbers. It's also about emotions. Because as much as we want to view finances as something rational, the reality is that they are deeply tied to how we feel. Debt, in particular, has a very strong emotional impact. And often, what drives us to go into debt isn't a real need, but rather a poorly managed emotion. What keeps us trapped in debt isn't just the interest or the bank, but the guilt, fear, or shame we feel about it. Therefore, if we want to use debt intelligently, we must also understand how it relates to our emotional world.

The most common emotion related to debt is stress. That constant weight of knowing you owe money and that you have to make payments month after month, sometimes without knowing if you'll be able to meet them. Financial stress doesn't just affect your wallet; it affects your health, your sleep, your mood. Many people live with a silent burden every day due to their debt. They wake up thinking about payments. They eat anxiously. They feel trapped. And the worst part is that they often don't talk about it with anyone. They keep it a secret. But like any emotion that isn't discussed, it accumulates. And stress isn't eliminated by avoiding the problem; it's reduced by confronting it with information and planning.

Another very common feeling is guilt. When someone goes into debt because of a bad decision, or because they spent money on something they couldn't pay off later, they start blaming themselves. They feel foolish, irresponsible, weak. This guilt can be so strong that it paralyzes them. Instead of looking for solutions, they mentally punish themselves. They say things like, "I was such an idiot," "I'm no good at managing money," "I've already ruined everything." And while it's good to admit a mistake, it's not healthy to live tied to guilt. We all make financial mistakes. We've all bought something we didn't need or taken out a loan without thinking it through. The important thing isn't to never make mistakes, but to learn and improve. Guilt doesn't pay off debt, but it can prevent you from facing it clearly.

There's also shame. This is a silent but very common feeling. The shame of owing money, especially when we feel others aren't in the same situation. Some people are ashamed to admit they're in debt, even to their partner, family, or friends. They think it makes them less successful, less responsible, less valuable. But the truth is, many people have debt, even those who seem to be doing very well. What you see on social media doesn't always reflect reality. Shame dissolves when you understand that debt doesn't define who you are. It's not a moral failing. It's a tool that's sometimes used well and sometimes misused. You don't have to hide because of it.

In some cases, debt is also linked to poorly managed positive emotions, such as euphoria or excitement. For example, many people go into debt for the excitement of a wedding, a party, or a trip. They spend more than they can afford because they're happy and don't want to limit that moment. What's understandable becomes dangerous when that emotion passes, leaving only the debt. It also happens when someone goes into debt to show love, buying expensive gifts or paying for things for others without having the money. The desire to please, to be accepted, or to avoid embarrassment can lead to poor financial decisions. It's necessary to learn to set limits, even when emotions are good. Because what seems like a nice gesture today can be an unnecessary emotional and financial burden tomorrow.

Another strong emotional connection to debt is fear. Fear of being foreclosed on. Fear of not being able to pay. Fear of losing your home. Fear of running out of credit. Fear can serve a useful purpose if it makes you take action and seek solutions, but it can also block you if you let it grow unchecked. Fear needs information to calm itself. It needs a plan. When you know exactly how much you owe, how you can pay it, and what options you have to refinance or negotiate, fear diminishes. The enemy isn't debt, it's uncertainty. And uncertainty is combated with clarity.

There are even people who go into debt to cover up other, deeper emotions, such as sadness, loneliness, or frustration. The act of shopping becomes a form of emotional escape. Going to the mall or shopping online gives them a sense of control or momentary pleasure. It's a quick anesthetic. But like any anesthetic, it wears off. And then comes the emotional hangover, when the bill arrives. That's why it's so important to be aware of why we buy what we buy. What need we're trying to fill. Because if the problem is emotional, the solution isn't financial. It's internal.

What many people need is not only a payment plan, but also self-compassion. Forgive yourself for your mistakes. Talk about your emotions without fear. Seek support if you need it. You are not alone in this. And you are not weak for feeling bad about debt. On the contrary, acknowledging how you feel is an act of courage. It's the first step toward doing things differently.

It's also important to talk to those you live with. Debt issues often affect a couple's relationship or family dynamics. If one person is in debt and doesn't talk about it, it can cause tension, arguments, or mistrust. But if both people share their emotions and their numbers, if they support each other and make a plan together, debt becomes manageable. Emotional and financial issues are always connected. Don't forget that.

In short, debt doesn't just take money; it can also affect your emotional well-being. But it doesn't have to be that way. You can use debt wisely and balanced if you also learn to manage the emotions surrounding it. Listen to what you feel. Name it. Don't beat yourself up for your financial mistakes. You are much more than a number. And if you take care of your mind and your heart, you'll be able to take much better care of your wallet. Because true financial freedom also begins within you.

Get Out of Debt Without Giving Up Living

Getting out of debt doesn't have to be a punishment. It doesn't mean you have to lock yourself in your house, stop enjoying yourself, forget about simple pleasures, or live as if you're grounded. Many people think that to get out of debt, you have to live on the edge, without coffee, without going out, without any joy. But that only leads to emotional exhaustion and, sooner or later, abandoning the plan. Because no one can endure for long living as if they're paying off a debt. And that's not the point. Getting out of debt must be a firm process, yes, but also a human one. And above all, sustainable. If your plan to pay off what you owe means you stop living, then you're very likely to abandon it at some point. We need a strategy that works, but that also allows you to enjoy the journey.

The first step is to calmly accept the situation. You're in debt, yes, but you're not trapped. There's a way out. Many people have done it before you, and you can do it too. But to achieve it without giving up your life, you need clarity and balance. Make a concrete list of everything you owe, with amounts, interest, and payment dates. Don't guess. Don't avoid it. Clutter only makes fear grow. Having that information on a spreadsheet or in an app is what will give you control. Without knowing exactly how much you owe, your mind invents monsters bigger than they really are.

Next, organize your spending. It's not about eliminating everything that brings you joy, but rather cutting back intelligently. You can continue to drink coffee, but maybe not every day outside the home. You can continue going out, but perhaps with a smaller, more conscious budget. The goal isn't to stop living, but rather to spend better. Often, it's not how much we spend, but on what. Some people spend without realizing it on things they don't even enjoy. Identify those empty expenses and cut them back. It's not about living with guilt, but with intention. Every peso not spent on unnecessary things can go directly to your freedom.

The next step is to create a payment plan that gives you breathing room. Don't set unrealistic goals. Don't say, "I'll pay it all off in three months" if it means skipping a meal or affecting your mental health. An effective plan is one you can follow month after month without feeling like you're drowning. If you have multiple debts, use the strategy that works best for you. You can pay off the smallest one first to see quick progress and motivate yourself, or you can focus on the one that generates the most interest to save more money in the long run. Both options are valid. The important thing is to move forward. Pay small but steady, like the trickle of water that eventually fills a whole bucket.

Another key point is to avoid isolation. Many people shut themselves away when they have debt, out of shame or fear. But this is the time when you need support the most. Talk to your family, your partner, someone you trust. You are not alone. You can even seek free or low-cost financial advice. There are institutions and professionals that can help you organize your payments, negotiate with creditors, or find better options. Sometimes a conversation can open a door you didn't see coming.

It's also important to celebrate progress. Although it may sound simple, marking a debt as paid on a spreadsheet or in an app can give you a sense of accomplishment that motivates you to keep going. Celebrate each step. You don't need to spend money to do it. It could be taking an afternoon off, watching your favorite movie, or inviting a friend over. These small celebrations remind you that the process isn't just about sacrifice, it's also about growth.

And don't forget that you can continue enjoying life, even if you're on a payment plan. There are many ways to have fun without spending money. A walk in the park, a chat with friends, cooking something delicious at home, reading a good book, listening to music. We sometimes confuse "living well" with "spending a lot." But they're not the same thing. Living well is enjoying life consciously, with peace, with gratitude. It's possible to have beautiful moments without spending money. And when you learn this, your finances improve on their own, because your happiness stops depending on your credit card.

Finally, take care of your mind. Paying off debt without giving up on life also means taking care of your emotional well-being. Don't punish yourself. Don't compare yourself. Don't call yourself a failure. We all go through difficult financial times. The key is how we face them. You're facing them bravely. You're reading, learning, making a plan. That's already a big step. And if you stay focused, while still giving yourself space to live, you'll emerge stronger, wiser, and freer.

Always remember this: paying off your debt is an act of self-love, not punishment. It's a way to free yourself, not limit yourself. You can move forward, while still enjoying the present. Because life doesn't pause while you pay. Life goes on. And you deserve to live it well, even while you build your financial freedom.

Live Free, but Not Allergic to Debt

For many years, many people have been taught to fear debt as if it were a contagious disease. As soon as they hear the word "credit" or "loan," they feel something is wrong. As if having debt automatically means failure or irresponsibility. In fact, some people proudly say they don't have a single credit card, that they don't owe a single cent, and that debt is a dirty thing to be avoided like the plague. And while it's admirable to live without unnecessary financial burdens, it's also dangerous to become allergic to all forms of debt, as if it were a deadly poison that destroys everything it touches. This mentality may seem healthy from the outside, but in reality, it limits growth, locks away opportunities, and leaves us off many paths that could lead us further.

Living free doesn't mean living isolated from the financial system. It means making informed decisions. And there are times in life when a loan can accelerate your growth. For example, if you're renting and find an affordable home that you could afford with a mortgage, perhaps that loan will be your springboard to building wealth. Or if your business is growing and you need a new machine to increase your production, a loan can give you the boost you couldn't achieve with your savings alone. It's like having a ladder in front of you, and for fear of tripping, you decide not to climb it. Of course, you have to be careful when climbing, but that doesn't mean you have to stay down forever.

The key is to see debt neither as an enemy nor as a savior. It's simply a tool. And like any tool, it can help or hurt you, depending on how you use it. If you take on debt without understanding the terms, without a plan, without knowing if you can pay it off, then yes, it becomes a problem. But if you use debt strategically, with clear goals, with financial education, and respect for your limits, then it becomes a powerful ally. You don't have to be afraid of it; you just have to know it well. Just as you don't fear a knife in the kitchen if you know how to use it, you shouldn't fear a credit card if you know how to manage it.

Many of life's important breakthroughs are achieved with the help of credit. Few people buy a house with cash or start a business without any financing. Even for college or a specialized degree, people often resort to a loan. If you close yourself off from all types of debt, you could also be closing yourself off from experiences that would make you grow. It's not about going into debt for everything, but rather opening the door to the possibility of using it wisely. Saying "no" to all debt can be as limiting as saying "yes" to all debt without thinking. Balance is what matters.

There are people who had bad experiences with debt, or saw their parents suffer from poorly managed loans, and that left a deep emotional mark on them. It's understandable. But the past doesn't have to dictate your future. If your experiences with debt weren't good, it doesn't mean they'll all be the same. You can relearn. You can educate yourself and see debt from a different angle. Information is what transforms fear into clarity. The more you understand about interest rates, terms, conditions, financial products, and money management, the less fear you'll feel and the more empowered you'll be.

Being free also means having options. And a person with a good credit history and who understands how debt works has more doors open to them. They can buy a property, they can access better banking products, they can get financing for a project, they can take advantage of an urgent opportunity without having to empty all their savings. That's true freedom: having the option to decide. Rejecting debt completely takes you out of the game, like someone who refuses to learn to drive because they once saw an accident. You can live without a car, yes, but you might go slower. And if you learn to drive well, that same car that once scared you can take you to places you'd never reach on foot.

It's not about becoming a credit fanatic, nor a card collector. It's about losing your fear of it through knowledge. Stopping to see it as something bad, and starting to see it as something you can master. Debt isn't synonymous with slavery if you have control. If you use it purposefully, if you understand its rules, if you know how to pay and when to say no, then not only will it not hurt you, but it can actually work in your favor. The problem isn't debt, the problem is not knowing what you're doing with that debt.

Living free is also living prepared. And part of being prepared in the modern world is understanding how finance, credit, and payment systems work. You can live a financially healthy life without being afraid of loans. You just need judgment, education, and responsibility. It's like riding a bike: it's scary at first, but once you learn, you can travel vast distances that would be impossible on foot.

So don't become allergic to debt. Be aware, yes. Be careful, too. But don't fear it as if it were an inevitable trap. You have the power to decide how to use it. And with that power, you can live truly free, not from fear, but from wisdom. Because true freedom is not rejecting everything that can go wrong, but knowing how to make things go right.

www.ingramcontent.com/pod-product-compliance
Lightning Source LLC
La Vergne TN
LVHW090422210926
848480LV00002B/654
* 9 7 9 8 2 3 0 7 7 1 4 8 7 *